Native American Life

The Great Plains Indians

Daily Life in the 1700s

by Mary Englar

Consultant:
Troy Rollen Johnson, PhD
American Indian Studies
California State University
Long Beach, California

Capstone press

Mankato, Minnesota

Bridgestone Books are published by Capstone Press,
151 Good Counsel Drive, P.O. Box 669, Mankato, Minnesota 56002.
www.capstonepress.com

Library of Congress Cataloging-in-Publication Data
Englar, Mary.
   The Great Plains Indians: daily life in the 1700s / by Mary Englar.
   p. cm.—(Bridgestone books. Native American life)
   Summary: "A brief introduction to Native American tribes of the Great Plains, including their
social structure, homes, food, clothing, and traditions"—Provided by publisher.
   Includes bibliographical references and index.
   ISBN 0-7368-4315-9 (hardcover)
   1. Indians of North America—Great Plains—History—18th century—Juvenile literature. 2.
Indians of North America—Great Plains—Social life and customs—18th century—Juvenile literature.
3. Great Plains—Antiquities—Juvenile literature. I. Title. II. Series.
E78.G73E54 2006
978.004'97—dc22   2005001635

Editorial Credits
Christine Peterson, editor; Jennifer Bergstrom, set designer; Ted Williams, book designer;
   Kelly Garvin, photo researcher/photo editor; maps.com, map illustrator

Photo Credits
Art Resource, N.Y./Smithsonian American Art Museum, Washington, D.C., 8
The Granger Collection, New York, 12, 16
Greenwich Workshop Inc./"Blackfeet Storyteller"/Howard Terpning, 20
North Wind Picture Archives, 18; Frederic Remington, 14
Stock Montage Inc./The Newberry Library, cover, 6, 10

1 2 3 4 5 6 10 09 08 07 06 05

Table of Contents

Great Plains
Tribal Areas in the 1700s

Sarcee

Plains Cree

Rocky Mountains

Blackfoot

Assiniboine

Plains Ojibwa

Gros Ventre

Hidatsa

Mandan

Crow

Arikara

Yanktonai Sioux

Teton Sioux

Missouri

Santee Sioux

Cheyenne

Yankton Sioux

Ponca

River

Omaha

Iowa

Pawnee

Arapaho

Missouri

Kansa

Wichita

Osage

Kiowa

Kiowa-Apache

Quapaw

Comanche

Mississippi River

Kichai

Tawakoni

Tonkawa

Scale
Miles
0   75   150   225   300

0   150   300
Kilometers

Legend

Mountain Range   River

4

The Great Plains and Its People

For thousands of years, Native Americans traveled the grassy prairies and rolling hills of the Great Plains. Today, this area covers central North America from the Rocky Mountains to the Mississippi River.

In the 1700s, Spanish explorers brought horses to the area. At that time, about 30 **tribes** lived on the Great Plains. Horses changed daily life for most tribes. Tribes were able to travel farther to hunt bison, also called buffalo. Most Great Plains tribes depended on buffalo for their daily needs.

◄ Great Plains tribes lived in the center of what is today the United States and Canada.

Social Structure

Great Plains Indians lived in family groups called **bands**. The families decided how many people lived in each band. They needed enough men to hunt and protect the group.

Bands also made up larger groups called tribes. Tribes sometimes formed larger nations. The Santee, Teton, Yankton, and Yanktonai tribes formed the Sioux Nation.

Chiefs and councils led tribes and made decisions for the people. Chiefs from different tribes met to talk about land, trades, hunting, and when to go to battle.

◀ Mandan leaders often gathered in the chief's home to make decisions for the tribe.

8

Homes

Most Great Plains Indians made **tepees** from wood poles and buffalo hides. Women sewed many hides together to cover the pole frames. Women built and owned the tepees.

In farming villages, people lived in their homes year-round. The Mandan built wood **lodges** with mud walls. Several families and their best horses lived in each lodge.

Farther south, the Wichita built small round houses. They covered wood frames with grass to build these homes. Thick layers of grass kept out the rain and wind.

◄ The Crow and other Great Plains tribes often decorated tepees with colorful paintings.

Food

The Great Plains Indians hunted buffalo in the spring and fall. Women dried extra meat for winter. They pounded dried meat into a paste and mixed it with fat. This **pemmican** lasted all winter.

As people traveled, they gathered wild berries and vegetables. They knew the best season to find each food.

Farming villages grew corn, beans, and squash. They traded extra crops for buffalo meat and hides.

◀ Tribes traveled across the Great Plains to hunt buffalo. People depended on the buffalo for food and clothing.

Clothing

Great Plains Indians made most of their clothing from animal skins. Women soaked deer or buffalo hides and scraped off any hair. Soft skins were used for shirts, leggings, and dresses. They used tough hides for the bottoms of moccasins.

Tribes often decorated their clothes. Blackfoot Indians used elk teeth to decorate shirts. The Cheyenne covered war shirts with paintings and porcupine quills. Many tribes sewed beads on their moccasins.

◄ The Sioux wore warm robes made of buffalo skins. They decorated clothes with paints made from plants.

Trading and Economy

For the Great Plains Indians, horses were a sign of wealth. Some Comanche warriors owned hundreds of horses. Tribes traded horses for food, hides, tools, and guns.

Hunting tribes brought hides and dried meat to farming villages. Mandan villages on the Missouri River traded corn, sunflower seeds, pottery, and baskets.

Large trading camps in Wyoming and North Dakota took place every year. Tribes often spoke different languages. They used sign language to make trades.

◀ Great Plains tribes used wooden carts called travois to carry goods to and from trading camps.

Leisure Time

Much of the year, the Great Plains Indians were busy with farming, hunting, and saving food for the winter. Children learned skills they would need as adults. Boys hunted rabbits and took care of the horses. Girls helped their mothers gather food and cook.

In their free time, tribes enjoyed playing games. Men and boys played a game called shinny. Shinny was played with a ball and stick. Players tried to pass the ball through a goal. Some tribes also played stickball. This game is also called lacrosse.

◀ Ball and stick games, like shinny and lacrosse, were popular games among Great Plains tribes.

Traditions

The Great Plains Indians respected nature and the land. They believed that the earth, sun, and sky had **spirits**. Some men danced to honor their promises to these spirits.

In spring, most tribes held a Sun Dance. The Sun Dance thanked spirits for good health and food. Singers and drummers performed as people danced.

Many tribes sent young men on **vision quests**. For many days, the men prayed alone. During prayer, they received a vision to help guide their lives and actions.

◄ Sioux leaders gave thanks to nature during ceremonies.

Passing On Traditions

The Great Plains Indians passed on their traditions through storytelling. Families gathered around elders to hear stories about the tribe's history. Children also learned about nature from the stories.

Some tribes painted pictures on buffalo hides to show important events. These hides were called **winter counts**. An artist added a new picture every winter. Paintings on one Kiowa winter count showed 60 years of the tribe's history. Winter counts help others learn about the tribe's past.

◀ Elders told stories to teach others about the tribe's past and way of life.

Glossary

band (BAND)—a group of Indian families that live and
hunt together

lodge (LODJ)—a permanent home made with a pole frame
and mud walls

pemmican (PEH-mi-kuhn)—dried buffalo meat mixed with
fat or fruit

spirit (SPIHR-it)—the nature of a person or animal; the soul.

tepee (TEE-pee)—a cone-shaped tent made of poles and
animal skins

tribe (TRIBE)—a group of people who share the same
language and way of life

vision quest (VIZH-uhn KWEST)—a time of prayer when
young men receive spiritual signs to guide their lives

winter count (WIN-tur KOUNT)—a picture history painted on
an animal hide

Read More

Kalman, Bobbie. *Life in a Plains Camp.* Native Nations of North America. New York: Crabtree, 2001.

Thompson, Linda. *People of the Plains and Prairies.* Native People, Native Lands. Vero Beach, Fla.: Rourke, 2004.

Internet Sites

FactHound offers a safe, fun way to find Internet sites related to this book. All of the sites on FactHound have been researched by our staff.

Here's how:
1. Visit *www.facthound.com*
2. Type in this special code **0736843159** for age-appropriate sites. Or enter a search word related to this book for a more general search.
3. Click on the **Fetch It** button.

FactHound will fetch the best sites for you!

Index